FITCHBURG PUBLIC LIBRARY

A1660275945 6

D0292048

This book was purchased
with state funds

■ Science Experiments for Young People ■

Environmental Experiments
About
LIFE

Thomas R. Rybolt
and
Robert C. Mebane

ENSLOW PUBLISHERS, INC.
Bloy St. and Ramsey Ave.   P.O. Box 38
Box 777   Aldershot
Hillside, N.J. 07205   Hants GU12 6BP
U.S.A.   U.K.

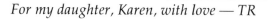

For my daughter, Karen, with love — TR

For Bob and Evie — RM

Acknowledgements
We wish to thank Mickey Sarquis, Ron Perkins, Richard Pekala, Clarence Murphy, and Robert Tate for their helpful comments on the manuscript, and Leah Rybolt for her assistance with two of the experiments.

Copyright ©1993 by Thomas R. Rybolt and Robert C. Mebane

All rights reserved.

No part of this book may be reproduced by any means without the written permission of the publisher.

Library of Congress Cataloging-in-Publication Data

Rybolt, Thomas R.
   Environmental experiments about life / Thomas R. Rybolt and
   Robert C. Mebane.
          p. cm. — (Science experiments for young people)
   Includes index.
       Summary: Uses experiments to explain ecosystems, life cycles, and
   interactions of life and environment including pollution and
   conservation.
       ISBN 0-89490-412-4
       1. Ecology—Experiments—Juvenile literature. 2. Life (Biology)—
   Experiments—Juvenile literature. 3. Pollution—Environmental
   aspects—Experiments—Juvenile literature. 4. Population—Juvenile
   literature. [1. Ecology—Experiments. 2. Life (Biology)
   —Experiments. 3. Pollution—Environmental aspects—Experiments.
   4. Population. 5. Experiments.] I. Mebane, Robert C. II. Title.
   III. Series: Rybolt, Thomas R. Science experiments for young
   people.
   QH541.24.R93   1993
   574.5′078—dc20   93-15582
                                                                              CIP
                                                                              AC

Printed in the United States of America

10 9 8 7 6 5 4 3 2 1

Illustration Credit: Kimberly Austin

Cover Illustration: ©John Shaw / Tom Stack and Associates

CONTENTS

series contents for
SCIENCE EXPERIMENTS
FOR YOUNG PEOPLE

ENVIRONMENTAL EXPERIMENTS ABOUT AIR
I. Oxygen and Carbon Dioxide
II. Our Protective Atmosphere
III. The Greenhouse Effect
IV. Air Pollution and Ozone
V. Dust

ENVIRONMENTAL EXPERIMENTS ABOUT WATER
I. Properties of Water
II. Water Cycle
III. Acid Rain
IV. Water Pollution
V. Water Purification

ENVIRONMENTAL EXPERIMENTS ABOUT LAND
I. Introduction to Soil
II. Properties of Soil
III. Land Changes and Erosion
IV. Recycling
V. Handling Wastes

ENVIRONMENTAL EXPERIMENTS ABOUT LIFE
I. Biodiversity and Ecosystems
II. Interactions of Life and Environment
III. Life Cycles
IV. Effects of Pollution on Living Things
V. Population and Conservation

Introduction

Earth

Earth, our home in space, has supported life for billions of years. But with a growing human population, people are having a greater effect on the environment than ever before. Together we must learn about the problems facing our environment and work together to protect the earth.

There are many ways we can work together to protect the earth. We can ask adults to use more fuel-efficient cars (cars that get more miles per gallon of gasoline). We can ride bikes or walk instead of getting rides in cars. We can recycle aluminum, paper, plastic, and glass, and we can plant trees. We can save energy by turning off lights when they are not in use. We can save energy by not keeping rooms and buildings too hot in the winter or too cold in the summer. Another way we can help the earth is to learn more about the environment.

This series of environmental books is designed to help you better understand our environment by doing experiments with air, water, land, and life. Each book is divided into chapters on topics of environmental concern or importance. There is a brief introduction to each chapter followed by a group of experiments related to the chapter topic. This series of environmental experiment books is intended to be used and not just read. It is your guide to doing, observing, and thinking about your environment.

By understanding our environment, we can learn to protect the earth and to use our natural resources wisely for generations to come.

Atoms and Molecules

Understanding something about atoms and molecules will help you understand our environment. Everything in the world around us is made of atoms and molecules. Atoms are the basic building blocks of all things. There are about 100 different kinds of atoms. Molecules are combinations of tightly bound atoms. For example, a water molecule is a combination of two hydrogen atoms and one oxygen atom.

Molecules that are made of only a few atoms are very small. Just one drop of water contains two million quadrillion, (2,000,000,000,000,000,000,000,000) water molecules.

Polymers are large molecules that may contain millions of atoms. Important natural polymers are natural rubber, starch, and DNA. Some important artificial polymers are nylon, which is used in making fabrics, polyethylene, which is used to make plastic bags and plastic bottles, and polystyrene, which is used in making styrofoam cups and insulation.

Atoms are made of smaller particles called electrons, protons, and neutrons. The nucleus is the center of the atom and contains protons and neutrons. Protons are positively charged, and neutrons have no charge. Electrons are negatively charged and surround the nucleus and give the atom its size.

Atoms and molecules that are charged are called ions. Ions have either a positive charge or a negative charge. Positive ions have more protons than electrons. Negative ions have more electrons than protons. Sodium chloride, which is the chemical name for table salt, is made of positive sodium ions and negative chlorine ions. Atoms, ions, and molecules can combine in chemical reactions to make new substances. Chemical reactions can change one substance into another or break one substance down into smaller parts made of molecules, atoms, or ions.

Science and Experiments

One way to learn more about the environment and science is to do experiments. Science experiments provide a way of asking questions and finding answers. The results that come from experiments and observations increase our knowledge and improve our understanding of the world around us.

Science will never have all the answers because there are always new questions to ask. However, science is the most important way we gather new knowledge about our world.

This series of environmental experiment books is a collection of experiments that you can do at home or at school. As you read about science and do experiments, you will learn more about our planet and its environment.

Not every experiment you do will work the way you expect every time. Something may be different in the experiment when you do it. Repeat the experiment if it gives an unexpected result and think about what may be different.

Not all of the experiments in this book give immediate results. Some experiments in this book will take time to see observable results. Some of the experiments in this book may take a shorter time than that suggested in the experiment. Some experiments may take a longer time than suggested.

Each experiment is divided into five parts: (1) materials, (2) procedure, (3) observations, (4) discussion, and (5) other things to try. The materials are what you need to do the experiment. The procedure is what you do. The observations are what you see. The discussion explains what your observations tell you about the environment. The other things to try are additional questions and experiments.

Safety Note

Make Sure You:

- Obtain an adult's permission before you do these experiments and activities.
- Get an adult to watch you when you do an experiment. They enjoy seeing experiments too.
- Follow the specific directions given for each experiment.
- Clean up after each experiment.

Note to Teachers, Parents, and Other Adults

Science is not merely a collection of facts but a way of thinking. As a teacher, parent, or adult friend, you can play a key role in maintaining and encouraging a young person's interest in science and the surrounding world. As you do environmental experiments with a young person, you may find your own curiosity being expanded. Experiments are one way to learn more about the air, water, land, and life upon which we all depend.

I. Biodiversity and Ecosystems

An ecosystem is the living and nonliving parts of the environment in a particular area. The whole surface of the earth may be thought of as one huge, extremely complex ecosystem. We call this ecosystem the biosphere. The biosphere includes the earth's air, water, and land that support life.

Having a wide variety of living things together in an ecosystem is called biodiversity. When species are destroyed and die out, then biodiversity is decreased. Each living thing is important because it fills a particular niche or role in some ecosystem.

The rain forest is one example of an ecosystem that is being threatened by the actions of people. As of 1992, over 160,000 square miles (415,000 square kilometers) of rain forest in South America had been destroyed due to actions such as burning the forest to make pasture for cattle, cutting all the trees down for timber, and digging up the land for mining.

As rain forests are destroyed, ecosystems in these areas are damaged, and biodiversity is decreased. Unique plants and animals, found nowhere else in the world, will die out completely. Just as every book in a library is unique and special, so every species (unique kind) of plant and animals is important. How would you feel if every copy of your favorite book were destroyed? If no one could ever again enjoy reading that book, it would be a great loss. In the same way, it is a great loss if species of life are destroyed and biodiversity is decreased due to the actions of people.

In the following activities, you will learn more about biodiversity by identifying unique living things and learn more about small ecosystems by studying life underneath a rock or log.

Experiment #1

How Many Species of Living Things Can You Find?

Materials

A pencil or pen

Sheets of paper

An area of land with a variety of living things (this could be a yard, a park, an area of woods, a vacant lot, or other spot of land)

Procedure

Have an adult help you identify as many different kinds of plants and animals as you can find. Write a brief description of each living thing or draw a simple picture of it. You may want to take a sample leaf from each plant to help you keep track of the types you have identified. ASK AN ADULT IF THERE ARE LIKELY TO BE ANY POISONOUS PLANTS, SUCH AS POISON IVY OR POISON SUMAC, AND HOW TO AVOID THESE. DO NOT DISTURB OR PICK UP ANY ANIMALS YOU MAY FIND. YOU SHOULD ONLY OBSERVE THEM.

You may want to spend several hours carefully look-ing along the ground, up in trees, under the soil, in the air, or wherever you can find living things. Look for things that seem obviously different than each other, such as plants with different shape leaves or birds with different color markings.

Observations

How many different kinds of living things are on your list? How many plants did you find? How many animals did you find? How many names of these living things did you know?

Discussion

Every area of land will have a different collection of living things so what you find will be unique. You may find only a few different living things or you may find hundreds, depending on where you look and how long you spend looking. You may be surprised by how many different living things can be found even in a small space.

More than one and one half million different species of life have been identified. Each species is a unique form of life with a special appearance and characteristics that makes it different from other species. Each species has the ability to produce more of its same kind. There is only one species of human beings, but there are about 1,000 species of fleas and more than 350,000 species of beetles. Individual species of life can be huge like the blue whale, which can grow to be 100 feet (30 meters) long. Other species of life, like protozoans, can be so small that they are invisible without the aid of a microscope.

Living things are sometimes divided into five large groups called kingdoms. These kingdoms include plant, animal, protist (algae and protozoans), moneran (blue-green algae and bacteria), and fungi (molds, mushrooms, and yeasts). However, in this experiment, we will simply refer to plants and animals. Plants produce their food from sunlight, use carbon dioxide from the air, and produce oxygen. Animals eat plants or other animals for food and release carbon dioxide to the air.

In 1735 a Swedish scientist named Carolus Linnaeus

published a classification of living things according to their structures. Individual species have unique characteristics that make them different than any other species. Biologists give each new species of life a unique name. However, you should find that you are often able to identify species that are different from each other even if you don't know any name.

Except for viruses, all living things are made of cells. Multicelled organisms like humans may contain billions and billions of cells working together. All living things share certain common building-block molecules and a similar genetic code that directs the production of the complex molecules that run the chemistry of the cell. The genetic code or molecular instruction manual for making and running a living thing is found in molecules of DNA (deoxyribonucleic acid).

Each species of life has unique DNA that helps make it different from any other species. Species of life are like books in a library. Each book in a library has a unique combination of letters and words that makes it different from all other books in the library. Just because there are many books in a library, we still would not want to lose any one book. Each book is special. In the same way, we do not want to lose even one species of living thing because each is special and unique.

Around the world, the activities of humans have threatened some species. These threatened species, such as the bald eagle, are called endangered species. Some species, such as the dodo bird, have been completely destroyed. Other species, such as the American bison, have been saved from extinction. The number of bison was reduced from probably 60 million in 1800 to less than 600 in 1889. Measures were taken to save the bison, and today there are about 20,000 in reserves around North America.

Other Things to Try

Field guides available from libraries and bookstores can help you identify the names of species of living things. These books are often based on a particular group of living things such as trees, birds, or insects. Use these guides or other books on plants and animals to learn the names and identify as many different plants and animals as you can. Keep a list of all the species of living things you observe.

Try to learn more about the living things you observe. Try to find out such things as their food or energy sources, their characteristics and appearances, their dependence on other living things, their habitats and niches, and their harms or benefits to people.

Find or make a bare patch of soil with no plants about twenty inches (fifty-one centimeters) on each side. Begin observing this spot of ground in spring. Observe the number and kind of plants and how these plants vary with time. A natural change over time in the species of life inhabiting an area of land is not uncommon.

Experiment #2

What Kinds of Animals Can You Find Under a Log or Rock?

Materials

A pencil or pen   Sheets of paper
An area of land with rocks or logs on the ground

Procedure

ALTHOUGH MOST ANIMALS YOU ENCOUNTER UNDER A ROCK OR LOG ARE HARMLESS, YOU SHOULD BE CAREFUL NOT TO TOUCH THEM. ALSO, DO NOT HARM ANY OF THE ANIMALS. Watch out for stinging insects like bees or wasps that may have nests in rotting logs or nearby. In some areas, there are poisonous snakes and scorpions that must be avoided. Most spiders are harmless to humans, but some spiders such as the black widow and brown recluse are poisonous.

Have an adult help you look on the ground around a rock or log and then use a stick to carefully turn over the rock or log. Closely examine the bottom of the rock or log and the ground underneath for animals. Write down the name or draw a picture of each different kind of animal you find. You can also write a brief description of each animal's color, size, and basic appearance.

Turn over several other rocks or logs and search for animals. After examining the rocks or logs, be sure to return them to the way you found them.

Observations

In what ways is the soil and ground underneath a rock or log different than the soil and ground around it? What kinds of animals do you find under the rock or log? Do you find these animals on the ground around the rock or log?

How many animals of each kind do you find under different rocks or logs? Do you know names of the animals you find?

Discussion

A habitat is a special location where a plant or animal lives. Each species or unique kind of plant or animal has a certain habitat or habitats where it lives. If a habitat is lost, a species of plants or animals may disappear or become extinct because it has no place to live.

The space under rocks and logs provides a type of habitat or living space for many animals. This habitat provides conditions that may be quite different than the uncovered ground immediately next to it.

The space under a rock or log may be different than the surrounding ground in several ways. The space under a rock or log is protected from sunshine and wind. It tends to be cool and damp under a rock or log since water does not evaporate easily from under a rock or log. These special conditions are sometimes called a microclimate. Also, the space is dark and provides some shelter from other animals that might eat them. Some animals may be more active outside the protected shelter at night when the surroundings of the rock or log are more likely to be cool, dark, and moist.

The microecosystem (an extremely small ecosystem) found under each rock or log may be somewhat different from other rocks and logs. There is no right answer of what you will find, but there are many possibilities.

Some of the animals you might find in an ecosystem under a rock or log include sow bugs (also called pillbugs or wood lice), slugs, snails, centipedes, millipedes, earthworms, spiders, earwigs, roaches, beetles, termites, ants, crickets, or larger animals such as lizards and salamanders.

The microecosystem under a rock or log provides a unique environment that gives a place for these animals to live. Some of these animals you may recognize as insects, such as roaches, crickets, beetles, and ants, which all have six legs. However, even within a single group, there are many possible species (unique kinds that reproduce their own kind). For example, there are more than 350,000 known species of beetles (the largest group of insects) and more are being discovered every year.

You will recognize centipedes and millipedes by their many legs. Centipedes tend to have long flattened bodies. Millipedes have long rounded bodies. A millipede looks like a worm with legs. Spiders have eight legs. Sow bugs, which are sometimes called pillbugs because some types can roll into a ball for protection, may not look much different than an insect. However, these fourteen-legged creatures are a type of crustacean more closely related to a lobster or crab than to an insect. Earwigs have pinchers on their abdomen. Snails have soft bodies with a shell. Slugs have soft bodies with no protective shell.

An ecosystem is the combination of the living and

nonliving things in the environment. Although the whole earth makes one extremely large ecosystem, it is common to divide the earth's area into large ecosystems called biomes. A biome is a community of plants and animals that covers a large land area sharing certain conditions such as temperature, rainfall, and altitude.

The rain forest biome, found in places like Brazil's Amazon jungle, is the richest biome in variety of life and the most threatened. Tropical rain forests are being destroyed at an alarming rate around the world. This biome is characterized by warm and wet weather and by an extremely great variety of species of plants and animals. As this biome is destroyed, many species of plants and animals may disappear.

Other Things to Try

Try to make a microecosystem by placing a board or log on the ground. Check under the board after one week to see if any animals have made a home there. Check again after several weeks and several months to see what changes have occurred.

Are there differences among the animals you find under rocks, fresh logs, and rotting logs? In a rotting log you may find ants, beetles, and termites cutting channels to live in the wood. You may find fungi living on the decaying material. How do differences in these environments affect the animals that live there?

II. Interactions of Life and Environment

It is clear that the ocean, atmosphere, geological systems, climate, and living things are interrelated and can affect each other. The earth is about four and one-half billion years old, and living things have been on the earth for more than three billion years. We know that greenhouse warming, acid rain, the ozone hole, and other problems of pollution in the atmosphere can affect the climate and weather. Pollution affects life on earth. However, life on earth also affects and helps control the nonliving parts of our world. For example, methane gas produced in the guts of cows and termites can contribute to greenhouse warming.

The interactions of the living and nonliving parts of our environment are extremely complex, and there is much we do not understand. However, we know that plants can affect animals and other plants. Animals can affect plants and other animals. Plants and animals can also affect and change their environments.

In these experimental activities, you will learn more about the role of living things on their environments, the effect of the environment on living things in the way they retain moisture, and how plants can influence animal behavior.

Experiment #3

Can Living Things Affect Their Environments?

Materials

A potato   Water
A knife
Hydrogen peroxide (3 percent solution)
Two small glass jars (baby food size works well)

Procedure

ASK AN ADULT TO HELP YOU WITH THIS EXPERI-MENT. READ THE LABEL ON THE 3 PERCENT HYDROGEN PEROXIDE SOLUTION. ONLY USE 3 PERCENT SOLUTION. DO NOT GET THIS SOLUTION IN YOUR EYES.

Have an adult cut off a thin piece of potato about the size of a quarter. Have an adult cut this piece of potato into four pieces. Place these slices of potato into a small glass jar and add enough water to completely cover them. Repeat this cutting procedure with another piece of potato. Place these pieces of potato into a second glass jar and add enough hydrogen peroxide solution to completely cover them. Watch both jars for several minutes.

Observations

Do you see bubbles of gas in the jar with water? Do you see bubbles of gas in the jar with the hydrogen peroxide? Are the bubbles of gas forming on the surface of the potato?

Discussion

You should observe bubbles of gas forming on the surface of the potato in the hydrogen peroxide solution. No bubbles should form on the potato placed in water.

Although the hydrogen peroxide solution is mostly water, it also contains a small amount of hydrogen peroxide. Each hydrogen peroxide molecule is made of two oxygen atoms attached to each other and two hydrogen atoms, one atom attached to each oxygen. A substance present in the cells of the potato causes hydrogen peroxide molecules to break apart to form molecules of water and oxygen. It takes two hydrogen peroxide molecules to form one oxygen molecule and two water molecules. The oxygen molecules combine to form the bubbles seen on the potato and in the solution. This substance that can break apart hydrogen peroxide molecules is called catalase.

Catalase is an enzyme. An enzyme is a large molecule present in living things. Enzymes are essential for life because they control the chemistry of living things. Without enzymes in cells, important chemical reactions would not occur. Hydrogen peroxide is made of only four atoms, whereas an enzyme like catalase is made of thousands of atoms. There are thousands of different kinds of enzymes in living things.

Catalase is present in cells to prevent the buildup of the hydrogen peroxide. One molecule of catalase can cause the breaking apart of five million hydrogen peroxide molecules every second. Hydrogen peroxide is formed sometimes when a cell obtains energy from food. However, hydrogen peroxide is toxic to cells and so must be removed, or it would accumulate and cause a breakdown of molecules in cells.

In this experiment, the potato that is exposed to hydrogen peroxide is changing its environment. There are many other situations where the living things on earth affect and help control their environment.

There have been some uses of bacteria and the

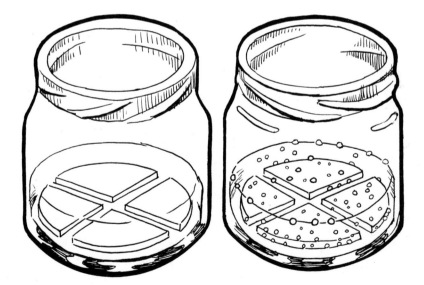

chemical reactions their enzymes cause to help clean up our environment. Bacteria and other simple life forms can be used to purify water by breaking down harmful molecules into safer forms. Bacteria and other living systems will probably be used more in the future to help control and treat pollution.

The gases in our atmosphere are one example of how living things affect the environment. The earth's atmosphere is about one-fifth oxygen and only a small amount of carbon dioxide. However, Venus, our neighbor planet, has an atmosphere that contains mostly carbon dioxide and no oxygen. There is no life on Venus and thus no plants producing oxygen through photosynthesis.

Billions of years ago, the early earth's atmosphere had very little oxygen. Oxygen in the atmosphere increased after photosynthesis of living things began to remove carbon dioxide from the air and release oxygen into the atmosphere. Blue-green algae and phytoplankton in the oceans as well as land plants produce oxygen that is used by animals. For the last 200 million years, the amount of oxygen in the atmosphere has remained quite constant.

Biological control helps maintain the earth's environment. Growing plants and animals change the environment where they are growing. For example, growing plants reduce carbon dioxide in the atmosphere.

James Lovelock, a British scientist, has proposed that

the entire earth is like a living organism, and he called this hypothesis Gaia after the Greek goddess of earth. Scientists disagree on the details of this idea but agree that living things affect the earth's environment. However, we do not fully understand all the complicated ways that living and nonliving parts of our world are interconnected.

Other Things to Try

Try repeating this experiment with different substances. Try adding plastic, sand, soil, carrot, ground beef (catalase has the highest concentration in blood and liver), cantaloupe, crushed leaves, and a broken twig to hydrogen peroxide solution. Make a record of which of these substances produce bubbles of oxygen when added to hydrogen peroxide.

What do your observations tell you about the presence of the catalase enzyme? What do your observations tell you about which of these are from living things?

Try cutting a potato into a series of small slices about the size of paper clips. Do you get more gas formed with a larger surface area of the potato exposed to the hydrogen peroxide solution?

Experiment #4

Is Water Important to Life?

Materials

Two firm apples of the same size
Vegetable peeler or small knife

Procedure

ASK AN ADULT TO REMOVE ALL THE PEEL FROM
ONE OF THE APPLES WITH A VEGETABLE PEELER
OR SMALL KNIFE. DO NOT USE A KNIFE BY YOUR-
SELF. Only the thin skin of the apple should be re-
moved. Save the apple peel.

Place both apples and the apple peel in a cool, dry
place where they will not be disturbed. Observe the
apples and the apple peel each day for a week.

After one week, ask an adult to cut each apple in half.
Observe what is different about the inside of the two
apples.

Observations

Does the peeled apple gradually become smaller and
softer than the unpeeled apple? Does the apple peel curl
up and become hard? Does the surface of the peeled
apple turn brown?

After you cut each apple in half, can you tell if there is more water in the peeled or unpeeled apple?

Discussion

Of all the chemical substances on earth, none is more important to plant and animal life than water. Although plants and animals contain many chemical substances, water is the most abundant substance. For example, a young person weighing 100 pounds contains about 60 pounds of water (60 percent water by weight). Some plants contain as much as nine pounds of water for each ten pounds they weigh (90 percent water by weight).

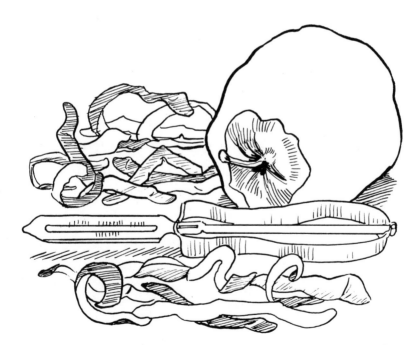

Water is important in life because nearly all the chemical substances that are used by a plant or animal to live and grow dissolve in water. Water also transports these chemical substances through the bodies of plants and animals where they are needed and used. Water also dissolves chemical substances that make up the waste products of plants and animals so that they can be easily removed.

Plants and animals have a protective coating covering their outside surface. Familiar examples include the bark on trees and the skin on animals. This protective covering is the boundary between the living organism and environment. One of the major purposes of this protective covering is to keep precious water inside the living organism. In addition, the protective covering guards the living organism against invasion by insects and microorganisms that could cause infection.

In this experiment, you are using apples to learn about the protective coverings of plants and animals. An apple is an example of a fruit. A fruit is the seed-containing part of a plant. The protective covering of the apple is the peel.

You should observe during this experiment that the peeled apple shrinks and becomes soft while the un-peeled apple does not shrink and remains firm. The peeled apple shrinks and becomes soft because water in the fleshy part of the apple escapes. The peeled apple is drying out. You should observe that the peel you re-moved also dries out.

The unpeeled apple does not shrink or become soft because its peel keeps the water in the fleshy part of the apple from escaping. The peel protects the apple from drying out.

The apple peel, like the protective coverings of other plants and animals, does not dissolve in water and is waterproof. Waterproof means water cannot pass through a substance or can only slowly pass through it.

Other Things to Try

Repeat this experiment for a longer time. Does the peeled apple continue to shrink?

Repeat this experiment with other fruits, such as pears, oranges, bananas, melons, tomatoes, and cucumbers. Do these fruits shrink when their peels are removed?

To show that the peel of an apple protects it from insects and microorganisms, place a peeled and an un-peeled apple outside on the grass for a week. Which one is attacked by insects first? Which one starts to rot first?

Experiment #5

Do Plants Produce Chemicals to Repel Insects?

Materials

An ant   Tabasco sauce

A plate   A spoon

A piece of paper

Procedure

ASK AN ADULT TO HELP YOU WITH THIS EX-
PERIMENT. Sprinkle Tabasco sauce in a ring near the
outer edge of a plate. Only a small portion of Tabasco
sauce will come out each time so it may take thirty or
forty drops of Tabasco to surround the plate. Use a
spoon to smear the Tabasco sauce around this outer
circle. There should be a continuous ring of liquid
making a circle around the plate. There should be no
Tabasco sauce in the center of the plate.

Carefully catch an ant and gently place it in the
middle of the plate. Watch the ant until it has come in
contact with the Tabasco sauce about eight times.
Now let the ant crawl on a piece of paper that you
hold in the center of the plate and return the ant to where
you found it.

Observations

Do you see the ant walk across the plate? What happens when the ant reaches the edge of the Tabasco sauce? How did the Tabasco sauce on the plate affect the ant's behavior?

Discussion

You probably observed that the ant walked across the plate until it came to the edge of the Tabasco sauce. When the ant reached the Tabasco sauce, it probably turned around and went in the opposite direction.

Again, the ant probably walked across the plate until it came to the edge of the liquid and turned around.

The ant may go back and forth stopping and changing its direction every time it comes to the edge of the Tabasco sauce. After several to a dozen encounters with the Tabasco sauce, the ant may finally walk through the sauce and off the plate.

Since plants cannot move to get away from insects or animals, they have evolved chemical means to repel or fight off insects. Plants produce a variety of special chemicals to help them grow and live. However, plants make other defense chemicals to help stop or slow attack by bacteria, fungi, insects, and other animals that could destroy the plants.

Capsaicin is a chemical found in hot cayenne peppers. These hot peppers are used in making hot sauces such as Tabasco sauce. Capsaicin is a natural insect repellent that helps prevent insects from eating and destroying pepper plants. The peppers repel insects because the insects try to get away from this irritating chemical.

The ant on your plate changed directions when it came close to the Tabasco sauce so it could get away from the capsaicin molecules that irritate it. The ant probably changed directions every time it got to the Tabasco sauce. However, after touching molecules of capsaicin a number of times, the ant may lose some of its sensitivity to this repellent and finally just walk through the Tabasco sauce.

There are many examples of natural chemicals that help protect plants: oil in the leaves of poison ivy, caffeine found in the coffee plant, and nicotine from tobacco plants. In higher concentrations, caffeine is a poison and nicotine has been used as an insecticide or chemical to kill insects. In fact, if the coyote tobacco plant is attacked by insects, this plant can concentrate enough poisonous nicotine so that one leaf has enough poison to kill ten rats. The attack of the insects causes the plant to produce a toxin to kill insects. Some plants even produce growth hormones that can change the speed of development of insects to keep them from reproducing.

We are only gradually beginning to understand how complicated the interactions are between living things in our environment. Some of these interactions are competitive, but many are mutually beneficial. Fungi growing on roots of some plants can help the host plant's roots better absorb water from soil. Microorganisms living in the digestive track of grazing animals can help them break down foods for nutrition. A type of ant that lives in the acacia plant found in South America feeds on juice from this plant but also protects the plant by stinging intruders that come near the plant.

Other Things to Try

Try repeating this experiment with an empty plate. Does the ant walk off the plate the first time it goes across? Try repeating this experiment with other substances, such as solid vegetable shortening (like Crisco) or vinegar, and compare the behavior of the ant.

Ask someone that raises a garden if they use any natural insect repellents. Some gardeners make a smelly spray from garlic and marigolds or plant marigold flowers to help keep harmful insects away. The oil in marigolds and garlic tends to repel insects. There are many repellent plants that help fight off specific insects. Some examples include nasturtiums to repel white flies and squash bugs, horseradish to repel potato bugs, oakleaf mulch to repel cutworms, tomatoes to repel cabbage maggots and cabbage moths, and eggplant to repel Colorado potato beetles.

Not all insects are pests. More than half of the 80,000 species of insects in North America are useful. These useful insects may aid in pollination of flowers or feed on other insects that destroy crops and garden plants. Ladybugs are insects that are good to have in a garden because they will eat more than twice their weight of aphids each day. A soap solution can be used to protect against some insects. Make a mixture of a tablespoon of dishwashing liquid in one gallon of water and spray it on plant leaves in a garden. This fights aphids and other insects that suck juices from plants.

III. Life Cycles

The biosphere of earth consists of three major parts. These are the hydrosphere, the lithosphere, and the atmosphere. The hydrosphere consists of all the water on earth, including the water in oceans, lakes, rivers, and the land. The lithosphere is the solid mineral material that covers the surface of the earth. The atmosphere is the blanket of air that surrounds both the hydrosphere and the lithosphere.

Together, the hydrosphere, lithosphere, and atmosphere contain all the chemical substances needed for life. The hydrosphere provides water, the lithosphere provides minerals, and the atmosphere provides oxygen, carbon dioxide, and nitrogen. Since there are limited amounts of these needed chemical substances, they must be used over and over again to keep life going.

The chemical substances required for life move through the biosphere in cycles. There are many cycles in the biosphere, and all of them are closely connected and depend on each other. Some important cycles include the carbon cycle, oxygen cycle, water cycle, nitrogen cycle, and mineral cycle. In the experiments that follow you will learn more about life cycles and how they work.

Experiment #6

What Happens to Grass When It Does Not Receive Sunlight?

Materials

A small, wooden board

Grass

Procedure

You should start this experiment in the morning on a sunny day. Place a small, wooden board on a patch of growing grass. Make sure to choose a spot where the grass is green and gets sun most of the day.

Raise the board in the late evening and observe the color of the grass. If the grass has started to turn yellow, completely remove the board from the grass. If the grass has not started to turn yellow, recover the spot of grass with the board. Check the grass under the board the next day in the late evening. Continue to keep the grass covered with the board until the grass starts to turn yellow. Depending on where you live and the type of grass you are using, it may take one day or several days for the grass to start to turn yellow.

Remove the board covering the grass when the grass

starts to turn yellow. Look at the grassy spot that was covered by the board each day for several days.

Observations

Does the grass covered with the board start to turn yellow after a day or two? Does the yellow grass turn green again after a couple of days?

Discussion

The pigment that gives leaves of green plants their color is called chlorophyll. In addition to chlorophyll, most green plants contain other pigments, including yellow

or orange pigments that are called carotenoids. The orange color of carrots is due to the carotenoid beta carotene. Normally, we do not see the carotenoid pigments or other pigments because the green chlorophyll pigment hides them. This is why the leaves of green plants appear green.

In green plants, chlorophyll plays a major role in photosynthesis. Photosynthesis, which means "putting together with light," is the process by which plants make their food. Through photosynthesis, plants make the sugar glucose from carbon dioxide and water. Plants obtain carbon dioxide from the air and water from the soil. Glucose is an energy-rich chemical substance. In addition to glucose, photosynthesis produces oxygen gas, which is released into the air by the plant.

The glucose made during photosynthesis is used by plants to make other important chemical substances needed for living and growing. Some of these chemical substances made from glucose include starch, cellulose, fats, various sugars, and proteins.

Sunlight supplies the energy for the photosynthesis process. Photosynthesis cannot occur in a plant that is deprived of sunlight. The plant is no longer able to make its food.

Chlorophyll is constantly being made in the leaves of green plants. However, the leaves of plants stop making chlorophyll when they are deprived of sunlight. Also, the chlorophyll already present in the leaves starts to break down. As the chlorophyll starts to break down and the green color fades, the yellow or orange carotenoid pigments can be seen in the plant's leaves. The carotenoid pigments take a longer time to break down in sunlight-deprived leaves.

In this experiment, you should observe that the grass covered with the board turns yellow after several days. The covered grass turns yellow because photosynthesis has stopped in the grass. The photosynthesis stopped because the grass was deprived of sunlight. The yellow color in the covered grass is due to the carotenoid pigments present in the grass.

When the yellow grass is again exposed to the sunlight, the yellow grass starts making chlorophyll again, and photosynthesis starts again. This is why the yellow grass should turn green after a couple of days in the sunlight.

In the autumn, when nights are cool and daylight becomes shorter, the leaves of some trees stop making pigments. Chlorophyll is the first pigment to break down. The fading of the green color exposes the red, yellow, or purple pigments that may also be present in the leaves. Eventually, all the pigments in the leaves break down, and the leaves turn brown.

Other Things to Try

Place a potted plant containing green leaves in a dark closet. Do the leaves start to turn yellow after a couple of days? Return the plant to a source of light when you are finished.

Experiment #7

Do Green Plants Make a Gas?

Materials

Water
A dead, dried-out, large, brown leaf
Three large, clear, glass jars with wide mouths
Two large, green leaves freshly picked from a tree, bush, or vine

Procedure

Ask an adult to help you pick the leaves. Make sure not to pick poisonous leaves such as poison ivy or poison oak leaves.

Fill three clear, glass jars nearly full with water. In one of the jars, place two, freshly picked, large, green leaves from a tree, bush, or vine. Gently shake the leaves while they are underwater to remove any air bubbles that may be sticking to the surfaces of the leaves.

Look at the green leaves carefully. Notice that the top and bottom are not the same. For this experiment, we will call the surface of leaves that normally face the sun the top surface. The bottom surface of leaves will be called the underside. When you place the green leaves in the water, make sure you can tell which side is the top surface and which is the underside.

Place a large, dead, dried-out brown leaf in the second jar. Leave the third jar empty. Gently shake the brown leaf while it is underwater to remove any air bubbles that may be sticking to the surfaces of the leaf.

Place the three jars in a window or outside where they will get plenty of sunshine.

Look at the jars after they have been in the sun for one hour. Observe both sides of the green leaves in the jar containing them. Observe both sides of the brown leaf in the jar containing it.

Gently shake the two green leaves while they remain underwater to remove any air bubbles on their surfaces.

Look at the levels in the two jars again after they have been in the sun for one more hour and make your observations.

Observations

Are there gas bubbles on the top surface and the underside of the two green leaves after one hour? Are there more gas bubbles on the top surface or the underside? Are there gas bubbles on the surfaces of the brown leaf?

Are there any gas bubbles on the inside surface of the jar of water that contains no leaves? Are there any gas bubbles on the inside surface of the jars that contain leaves?

Do gas bubbles appear again on the underside of the two green leaves after the gas bubbles that formed on

the underside during the first hour were removed by
gently shaking the leaves?

Discussion

Photosynthesis is the process by which green plants
capture and store the sun's energy. Green plants capture the sun's energy by absorbing sunlight with their
leaves. They store this absorbed energy by using it to
make chemical substances that are rich in energy.
These energy-rich chemical substances made by
plants are called carbohydrates and include sugars

and starches. Plants use carbohydrates to make other chemical substances they need to live and grow.

Photosynthesis is the way that energy from the sun is introduced into the world of life. Unlike green plants, animals cannot use the sun's energy to make energy-rich chemicals they need to live and grow. Instead, animals obtain energy from the sun indirectly by eating plants or by eating animals that eat plants.

Plants make carbohydrates from simple chemical substances. These simple chemical substances are carbon dioxide and water. Plants obtain the carbon dioxide from the air and the water from the soil.

In addition to carbohydrates, a second important chemical substance is produced by green plants during photosynthesis. This chemical substance is oxygen gas. The oxygen gas made by plants is released into the air and becomes part of the atmosphere.

In this experiment, the bubbles you see on the underside of the two green leaves submerged in the jar of water is oxygen gas. This oxygen gas is made by the leaves as the leaves carry out photosynthesis.

Plants take in carbon dioxide needed for photosynthesis from the air through tiny openings on their leaves. These tiny openings on leaves are called stomata. Oxygen gas made during photosynthesis is also released into the air through the stomata of leaves.

Interestingly, most of the stomata in leaves are found on the underside of leaves. This is why you should notice that most of the gas bubbles are on the underside of the green leaves in your experiment.

You should not observe any gas bubbles on the dead brown leaf submerged under water. The dead leaf cannot carry out photosynthesis. If you do see some tiny gas bubbles on the dead brown leaf or in the jar containing just water, air that was dissolved in the water at the beginning of the experiment has changed back into a gas.

Animals need oxygen to live. Animals use oxygen to release energy stored in energy-rich foods such as carbohydrates and fats. This release of energy is called respiration. Animals use the energy released in respiration to live and grow.

Just like animals, plants take in oxygen and use it to release energy by the process of respiration. Plants use respiration to release the energy stored in energy-rich foods like carbohydrates they make during photosynthesis.

At night, plants take in oxygen from the air for respiration. During the day, plants do not need to take in oxygen from the air because photosynthesis supplies all the oxygen needed by the plants. Considerably more oxygen is produced by photosynthesis than is needed by plants. This excess oxygen is released into the atmosphere to replenish the oxygen used during respiration by animals and plants.

Photosynthesis and respiration are part of two

important cycles in life, the carbon cycle and the oxygen cycle. In the carbon cycle, carbon cycles between carbon dioxide and energy-rich chemical substances like carbohydrates. Carbon dioxide is changed into carbohydrates by photosynthesis. During photosynthesis oxygen is also made, which is then used during the respiration of living things to release the energy stored in carbohydrates. It is during respiration that oxygen becomes combined with carbon in the carbohydrates to form carbon dioxide and the cycles repeat. Although difficult to measure accurately, it has been estimated that 800 trillion pounds of carbon dioxide are cycled annually via photosynthesis and respiration.

Other Things to Try

Eventually the leaves submerged under water no longer generate oxygen gas because they run out of carbon dioxide. How long does this take?

To show that light is necessary for photosynthesis, repeat this experiment at night. Do you still see bubbles form on the underside of the leaves?

Experiment #8

Do Plants Use Carbon Dioxide?

Materials

Water

Aluminum foil

Measuring cup

Dark closet

Felt-tip pen

Freshly picked, green leaves

Three one-gallon, zipper-close plastic bags

Baking soda

A large bowl

Measuring spoon

Tape

Procedure

Place a piece of tape on each plastic bag. Label one bag "baking soda/light," another "baking soda/dark," and the last bag "water only."

Add one teaspoon of baking soda to the bag labeled "baking soda/light" and to the bag labeled "baking soda/dark." Add eight cups of water to each of these two bags, seal the bags, and shake the bags to dissolve the baking soda in the water. Add eight cups of water to the bag labeled "water only."

Place two, large, freshly picked, green leaves in each of the three bags. Ask an adult to help you pick the leaves. Make sure not to pick up poisonous leaves such as poison ivy or poison oak leaves.

Squeeze all the air out of the bags and then seal the bags. If there is still some air in the bags, open one corner of the bag slightly and squeeze the air out. However, make sure none of the bags will let water leak out.

Place two pieces of aluminum foil slightly larger than a gallon zipper-close plastic bag next to each other outside on the ground. Choose a spot that gets plenty of sunlight.

Place the bag labeled "baking soda/light" on one of the pieces of aluminum foil and the bag labeled "water only" on the other piece of aluminum foil. Put the bag labeled "baking soda/dark" in a large bowl and place the bowl in a dark closet.

Observe the leaves in all three bags after one hour. Gently shake each bag to dislodge any gas bubbles sticking to the leaves.

Repeat your observations several times during the day making sure to gently shake each bag to dislodge any gas bubbles sticking to the leaves. Continue the experiment for two days.

Observations

Are there more gas bubbles on the underside of the green leaves in the bag labeled "baking soda/light" than on the underside of the leaves the bag labeled "water only" after one hour?

During the two days you do this experiment, does more gas collect in the bag labeled "baking soda/light" than in the bag labeled "water only?" Does any gas collect in the bag labeled "baking soda/dark" during the two days?

Discussion

The gas that forms on the leaves and collects in the two bags placed in the sunlight is oxygen. Oxygen is one of the products of photosynthesis, which takes place in the leaves. Photosynthesis is the way in which green plants make their food and ultimately all the food available on earth.

In photosynthesis, carbon dioxide and water combine to make glucose. Glucose is a simple sugar that is a type of carbohydrate. Carbohydrates are

energy-rich chemical substances and are found in many foods.

It takes six carbon dioxide molecules and six water molecules to make one molecule of glucose. Each time a glucose molecule is made from six carbon dioxide molecules, six oxygen molecules are also made. The oxygen gas made during photosynthesis is released into the air through a plant's leaves. The glucose stays in the plant and is used by the plant as a source of energy to make other important chemical substances.

Photosynthesis requires energy. This energy comes from sunlight. Plants can only carry out photosynthesis during the day when the sun is shining. Plants do not carry out photosynthesis at night or in the dark. You should observe that no gas bubbles form on the leaves or are collected in the bag labeled "baking soda/dark" during the entire experiment. No gas was formed because the leaves were kept in the dark.

Plants obtain the carbon dioxide they need for photosynthesis from the air. Air contains about three hundredths of a percent of carbon dioxide (0.03 percent). This means there are approximately three carbon dioxide molecules out of every ten thousand molecules in the air.

Plants take in carbon dioxide from the air through tiny holes called stomata that are located on their leaves. The oxygen made during photosynthesis is also released through the stomata of leaves. Interestingly, most of the stomata of leaves are located on the underside of the leaves. You can tell this is the case with the leaves in two bags placed in the sun. You should observe more gas bubbles on the underside of these leaves than on the top side.

You should observe that more oxygen gas bubbles form on the leaves and are collected in the bag labeled "baking soda/light." This means the leaves in the bag labeled "baking soda/light" have carried out more photosynthesis than the leaves in the bag labeled "water only." More photosynthesis has been carried out by the leaves in the bag labeled "baking soda/light" because there is more carbon dioxide available to the leaves in this bag.

Baking soda is a source of carbon dioxide. The water in the bag labeled "baking soda/light" has baking soda dissolved in it. The bag labeled "water only" does not contain any baking soda. This is why there is more carbon dioxide available to the leaves in the bag labeled "baking soda/light." And since there is more carbon dioxide available to these leaves, more glucose and oxygen gas can be made by these leaves during photosynthesis.

It is known that plants generally grow better in air containing more carbon dioxide than is naturally present. This is because more carbon dioxide is available to the plants for carrying out photosynthesis. Interestingly, some greenhouses maintain an atmosphere containing two to five times more carbon dioxide than the amount of carbon dioxide in the natural atmosphere.

Scientific research is currently being conducted to predict the effect on green plants of increasing amounts of carbon dioxide in our atmosphere due to the burning of fossil fuels. In one study, researchers found that pine and aspen trees in a natural forest environment with an atmosphere containing twice the normal amount of carbon dioxide weighed on average 20 percent more than pine and aspen trees grown in a normal atmosphere. It was found that trees grown in the carbon dioxide-rich atmosphere also had more leaves and bigger leaves. Future research studies should increase our understanding of the effect of rising atmospheric carbon dioxide levels and global warming on the growth of plants.

Other Things to Try

Repeat this experiment using different kinds of leaves. Try bigger leaves. Try smaller leaves.

Repeat this experiment with dead, dried-out leaves. What are your results?

Experiment #9

Are Nitrogen and Other Nutrients Needed for Plant Growth?

Materials

A measuring cup   Measuring spoons

A large jar   Water

A permanent marker   Ryegrass seed

Long-handled, metal spoon

Four small, glass jars (baby food size)

White sand (type used in sandboxes)

Fertilizer (Miracle-Gro water-soluble 15-30-15 plant food)

Procedure

HAVE AN ADULT HELP YOU WITH THIS EXPERI-MENT. DO NOT GET THE FERTILIZER ON YOUR SKIN OR IN YOUR EYES. Carefully wash all measuring spoons when finished.

Pour four cups of water into a large jar. Add one-fourth teaspoon of powdered fertilizer to the water in the jar and stir until well mixed. This mixture of fertilizer and water is a fertilizer solution. You will only use a small portion of this fertilizer solution. You can use the extra fertilizer solution on other plants that may need fertilizing.

Use a permanent marker or use a piece of tape and a felt pen to label each small jar as either "1," "2," "3," or "4." Sprinkle one-half teaspoon of sand to cover the seeds in each jar.

Add two teaspoons of water to jar "1." Add one teaspoon of water and one teaspoon of fertilizer solution to jar "2." Add two teaspoons of fertilizer solution to jar "3." Jar "4" will have the most fertilizer. Add one-quarter teaspoon of fertilizer powder and two teaspoons of water to jar "4." Jar "4" has as much fertilizer as the whole jar of fertilizer solution.

Set these jars in a sunny spot where they will not be disturbed. Each day add about one-half to one teaspoon of water to each jar. Add enough water to keep the sand moist but not so much water to make the sand float and flood the seeds. Add the same amount of water to each jar. Compare the jars each day for at least one week.

Observations

In which jar does the grass first come up above the sand? In which jar does the grass grow the fastest? After one week, which jar has the tallest grass? Which jar has the second and third tallest grass? Is there a jar with no grass growing?

Discussion

You probably will find that the grass in jar "3" came up above the sand first and grew the fastest. After one week, the grass in jar "3" is probably taller than the grass in jar "2." The grass in jar "2" may be taller than the grass in jar "1." You may also find that the number of blades of grass growing increases as the amount of fertilizer solution increases from jar "1" to "2" to "3." However, the grass in jar "4" probably did not grow.

Up to a point, the more fertilizer added, the better the grass grows. However, too much chemical fertilizer can damage plant roots and kill useful microorganisms in the soil. In your experiment, the grass in jar "4" that was greatly overfertilized should not grow.

The nutrients that are essential for plant growth include primarily nitrogen, phosphorus, and potassium. Smaller amounts of thirteen other elements, such as zinc, iron, copper, and sulfur, are also needed. The fertilizer used in this experiment is 15-30-15, which is a measure of the equivalent percents of nitrogen, phosphorus, and potassium.

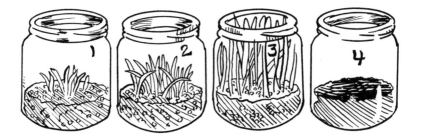

Nitrogen is important because nitrogen atoms are part of chlorophyll molecules used in plant photosynthesis. Nitrogen is also part of protein molecules that are important in plant growth and regulation. Lack of nitrogen makes older leaves turn yellow and the plant fails to grow.

Phosphorus is important to help roots, fruit, and flowers grow. Plants with not enough phosphorus are often small and may have discolored leaves with slow development of fruit.

Potassium is important to help make and move starch and sugar molecules within a plant. Potassium is necessary for plants to develop seeds, fruit, and flowers. Plants without enough potassium have dry leaves and dead areas on the plant and are smaller than expected.

Although air is mostly nitrogen, most plants cannot use pure nitrogen directly from the air. Nitrogen in air must first be changed into a nitrogen-containing chemical compound called ammonia. This process is called nitrogen fixation. Fixed nitrogen, such as ammonia, is used by the plants to grow. When plants and animals die and decay, they return their nitrogen compounds to the soil for other growing plants to use.

To get the maximum crop yield from available land, farmers use chemical fertilizers to put more nitrogen and other nutrients into the soil. Farmers may add ammonia and allow bacteria in the soil to convert the ammonia to nitrates. Or they may apply fertilizers containing nitrates directly to the soil.

Although use of fertilizers has helped increase crop yields dramatically, the heavy use of nitrogen fertilizer also can have damaging environmental consequences. Rainwater runoff from crop land can carry fertilizer containing nitrates and phosphates into lakes and damage the ecosystem by causing too much algae growth in a process called eutrophication. The algae may cover the lake in a green scum, and when the algae dies, it decays on the bottom of the lake. Bacteria that feed on the decaying plants use up the oxygen in the lake. Other aquatic organisms like fish and water snails die for lack of oxygen.

Other Things to Try

Try repeating this experiment with different amounts of fertilizer and water to find the strength of fertilizer solution that can make the grass grow the fastest.

Using two planting pots, fill one with sand and the other with potting soil. Plant an equal number of grass seeds in each pot and add water daily as needed to keep soil and sand moist. Compare the growth of the grass in the two pots. Not only does the soil have nitrogen and other nutrients needed by the plant, but the soil is also better at retaining water and air needed by the growing plant.

IV. Effects of Pollution on Living Things

Pollution is a serious problem in many parts of the world. Two major types of pollution are air pollution and water pollution. Most air pollution is caused by power stations and industries that burn fossil fuels such as coal and oil to produce energy and to make materials we use. Automobile exhaust is also a large source of air pollution. Major sources of water pollution are sewage, industrial wastes, runoff of agricultural fertilizers and pesticides, oil spills, and seepage from landfills and septic tanks.

Pollution can be harmful in many ways. It can cause health problems for people and animals, particularly among the elderly and the very young. Pollution can damage plants and reduce crop yields. Buildings, clothing, and other objects can also be damaged by pollution. Besides being harmful, pollution can smell bad and make things dirty.

In the experiments that follow, you will learn how acid rain and air pollutants can harm and even kill plants. You will also learn about indoor air pollution and how it can be harmful to people. Finally, you will learn how oil spills harm aquatic birds and mammals.

Experiment #10

Does Acid Rain Have an Effect on Plants?

Materials

A measuring cup	Water
Vinegar	Measuring spoons
Tape	Felt-tip pen
A patch of growing grass	
A trowel or small shovel	
Two small, glass jars (baby food size)	

Procedure

Have an adult help you dig up two small patches of grass sod. These pieces of grass sod should include the roots and attached soil. Each patch should be about the size of the glass jars you are using.

Put a piece of tape on the first jar and write "water" on the tape.

Add one-eighth cup of water to the first jar and push the piece of grass sod into the jar. The clump of grass sod should be pushed down into the bottom of the jar so that the soil is mixed with the water.

Add one-eighth cup of vinegar to the second jar. Push the piece of grass sod into the bottom of the jar so that the soil is mixed with the vinegar.

Set the two jars filled with grass in a w
spot where they will not be disturbed for

Observations

Compare the clumps of grass each day for about four days. Write down any differences you see between the grass in each jar.

Discussion

Excessive acid can kill living things such as grass. You probably observed that the grass in the vinegar slowly turned from green to brown. The brownness spreads from the roots up toward the leaves. The tips of the

blades of grass remain green while the bottom is brown. Over several days, the grass in the vinegar will probably turn completely brown. The grass in the water should continue to be green and grow.

Vinegar is a mixture of acetic acid in water. Vinegar is much more acidic than normal tap water. The excessive acid in vinegar can kill growing grass.

It is normal for lakes and rivers to be slightly acidic because of natural acids. However, pollutant molecules such as sulfur dioxide and nitrogen oxide can cause rain and snow to become more acidic than is normal. Sources of these pollutant molecules include burning coal that contains sulfur and running automobile engines. These pollutant molecules cause acids to form in the atmosphere. This excessive or extra acidity in precipitation is called acid rain.

Water can be acidic, neutral, or alkaline depending on what chemicals are in the water. Different living things can only live within a certain range of acidity. Aquatic life in lakes and rivers can be harmed by acid rain that makes the water too acidic for the living things to survive.

There are some lakes that have clear beautiful water but are dead lakes. In these dead lakes, all the living things in the lake, including the algae or green plants that give water a cloudy appearance, have been killed. To stop acid rain from harming lakes, it is necessary to reduce the amount of pollutant molecules that cause acid rain.

Lime or limestone is sometimes added to lakes and ponds to make them more alkaline and less acidic. Adding lime or limestone can keep ponds and lakes from becoming too acidic. This may help control the acidity of lakes until the sources of acid rain are stopped.

Other Things to Try

Try repeating this experiment but mix together different amounts of water and vinegar. Is there a minimum amount of vinegar that causes the grass to die? Does the amount of vinegar affect how fast the grass changes from green to brown?

Add a teaspoon of baking soda to one-eighth cup of vinegar and repeat this experiment. Adding baking soda, which is an alkaline substance, is similar to liming a lake. If you add enough baking soda, you can neutralize the acid, and the grass should grow without being killed.

Have an adult go with you to collect water from a small pond. DO NOT GO NEAR A POND OR BODY OF WATER WITHOUT AN ADULT. You need to find a pond or small body of water that has a thick, green growth of algae. By having a thick growth of algae, you will be able to see changes if the algae dies. Pour the pond water into several small jars and add different amounts of vinegar to each jar. Let the jars sit in a sunny spot for several days and watch for any changes in the green pond water. If you add enough vinegar to pond water, it will cause the water to become so acidic that all the algae could be killed. You can repeat this experiment with other types of acids, such as lemon juice.

Thoroughly wet one paper towel with water and a second paper towel with vinegar. Place six lima beans on each paper towel and fold the towels in half to cover the beans. Place each paper towel in a jar and check both after about four days. Do the seeds in the water germinate (begin to grow)? Do the seeds in the vinegar begin to grow?

Experiment #11

Does Sulfur Dioxide Harm Plants?

Materials

Tape

Felt-tip pen

A paper towel

Fresh spinach leaves

A "strike anywhere" match and match box

Two clean, dry, clear, glass jars with tight-fitting lids

Procedure

ASK AN ADULT TO HELP YOU WITH THIS EXPERI-
MENT. DO NOT USE MATCHES BY YOURSELF!

This experiment works best on a bright, sunny day.

Fresh spinach leaves are available in most supermar-
kets year-round. Choose two spinach leaves that are
about the same size and color. The leaves should fit
easily in the glass jars. Dry the spinach leaves with a
paper towel if they are wet or damp.

Place a piece of tape on the lids of each jar. Write
"sulfur dioxide" on one piece and "control" on the
other.

Place the match box next to the jar labeled "sulfur
dioxide." Remove the lid from the jar. The adult should
strike a match on the match box and quickly place the
match in the jar. Immediately tighten the lid on the jar.

The match may still be burning when you tighten the lid on the jar. It will soon stop burning.

After the match has stopped burning, unscrew the lid on the jar labeled "sulfur dioxide" and place a piece of spinach leaf in the jar. Quickly retighten the lid on the jar. Place a piece of spinach in the jar labeled "control" and tighten the lid on this jar.

Place the jars with their sides down on a flat surface outside on a spot that gets plenty of sunshine. Observe the spinach leaves in each jar every hour for three hours. After three hours, remove the spinach leaves from the jars and look at them closely.

Observations

Do you notice any change in the spinach leaves in either jar after they have been in the sunlight one hour? Is the leaf in the jar labeled "sulfur dioxide" turning a light color? After two hours, do you notice any change in the spinach leaves? After three hours, what changes have taken place in the color of the spinach leaves?

Discussion

Sulfur dioxide is a colorless, sharp-smelling gas. Sulfur dioxide is a major air pollutant. This gas can harm both plants and animals. It is produced during the burning of fossil fuels that contain sulfur. Examples of such fuels include coal, gasoline, and heating oil.

In this experiment, you are exploring how sulfur

dioxide harms plants. You are making the sulfur dioxide for the experiment from a "strike anywhere" match. When the tip of this kind of match is rubbed on a surface, friction causes chemicals in the tip to undergo a chemical reaction with oxygen in the air to produce enough heat energy to cause a flame. One of the chemicals in the tip of the match contains sulfur, which changes to sulfur dioxide in the reaction. The characteristic smell of lighting a match is due to sulfur dioxide.

Sulfur dioxide harms plants by destroying living tissue in a plant's leaves and stems. Sulfur dioxide enters the leaves of plants through tiny openings on the leaves called stomata. These tiny openings are used by the plant to exchange gases, such as oxygen, carbon dioxide and water, with the air.

When sulfur dioxide enters the stomata, it damages living cells in the leaves. The leaf turns brown in spots.

If the damage is great, the leaf can die. If enough leaves on a plant die, then the plant can die.

Sulfur dioxide does most of its damage to the leaves of plants during the middle of the day. The stomata of leaves are open the widest at this time of the day. At night the stomata close.

You should observe the spinach leaf in the jar labeled "sulfur dioxide" turns light brown in color. This is because the sulfur dioxide you made with the match is entering the stomata of the spinach leaf and damaging tissue inside the leaf. The leaf in the jar labeled "control" should not change color.

Not only can sulfur dioxide damage living tissue, it can be changed in the atmosphere into sulfurous and sulfuric acids, which can return to earth as acid rain or snow. Nitric acid, which is made in the atmosphere from the pollutant nitrogen dioxide, is another acid that makes acid rain and snow.

Other Things to Try

Repeat this experiment at night. Do you get similar or different results? Why?

Repeat this experiment using other fresh vegetable leaves, such as cabbage, turnip, mustard, and lettuce.

Try this experiment with fresh leaves from trees. Are some leaves more sensitive than others?

Repeat this experiment with fresh pine needles. What do you observe?

Experiment #12

What Is Indoor Pollution?

Materials

A new, white, styrofoam cup
Scissors

Procedure

Smell the outside of the styrofoam cup. Use the scissors to quickly, but carefully, cut out a piece of styrofoam from the cup about the size of a postage stamp. Quickly smell the small piece of styrofoam along the edges where it was cut with the scissors. Place the small piece of styrofoam on a table where it will not be disturbed. Smell the small piece of styrofoam again after ten minutes.

Observations

Does the uncut styrofoam cup have a distinctive odor? Does the cut piece of styrofoam have a smell after ten minutes?

Discussion

Indoor air pollution can be as bad as air pollution out-doors. In buildings and homes that are tightly sealed to save energy, indoor air pollution can be even worse since the pollutants are trapped inside.

Some of the same pollutants found in air pollution outdoors can be found in indoor air pollution. These pollutants include nitrogen oxides, carbon monoxide, and hydrocarbon vapors. The nitrogen oxides and carbon monoxide can be formed from gas ranges, kerosene space heaters, malfunctioning furnaces, and water heaters that burn fossil fuels. Hydrocarbon vapors can come from oil-based paints and paint thinner. Other possible indoor air pollutants are asbestos fibers, radon gas, cigarette smoke, and household chemicals such as pesticides. One way to rid a house or building of indoor

pollutants is to open windows and doors and let the inside air out.

Homes and buildings that have formed insulation may have a problem with formaldehyde vapors. Formaldehyde vapors can also be released from certain adhesives found in carpeting and building materials like plywood, paneling, and particleboard. Formaldehyde is a toxic gas that can cause skin and eye irritation, nausea, and other serious health problems.

Foamed insulation is a polymer. A polymer is a large molecule made by joining together smaller molecules called monomers into long chains. The smaller molecules joined together in foamed insulation are sometimes formaldehyde and urea. When foamed insulation of this type is made, some formaldehyde molecules do not form a polymer. These formaldehyde molecules can become trapped in the foam. Over a period of time, the formaldehyde molecules can move to the surface of the foam and then move into the air as a gas.

The release of a gas by a foam is called outgassing. Outgassing occurs more readily in new foamed insulation and can last for years. Outgassing can also occur with adhesives made with formaldehyde.

In this experiment, you are using a styrofoam hot drink cup to show that foams can contain unreacted monomer molecules. Styrofoam is a foam product made from the polymer polystyrene. Polystyrene is made by joining styrene molecules together in long chains. Some styrene molecules do not join to make a polymer and become trapped in the polymer.

The outside of the styrofoam should not have any smell. The piece of styrofoam that was cut from the cup should have a faint but characteristic smell. This smell indicates the presence of styrene molecules. Some of the odor could be due to chemicals that are used to put gas in the foam to make styrofoam light. These molecules can also contribute to indoor pollution by outgassing. After ten minutes, the piece of styrofoam should not have a smell around where it was cut because the styrene molecules on the surface of the cut move into the air.

Other Things to Try

Repeat this experiment with other materials made of styrofoam.

Have you ever smelled the inside of a new car? The smell of a new car is due to a chemical added to the plastic materials in the car. This chemical outgasses and gives new cars an odor. After a period of time, this chemical in the plastic all outgasses and in older cars can no longer be smelled.

Experiment #13

How Can Oil Spills Harm Animals?

Materials

Four clean cotton balls   Cooking oil

Two large ice cubes   Three small plates

Two zipper-close plastic bags

Procedure

Place a large ice cube in each plastic bag. Squeeze as much air out of the bags as you can and seal the bags. Place one bag on the first plate and the second bag on the second plate.

Pour cooking oil on two of the cotton balls until the cotton balls are nearly full with the oil. Place one of the oil-soaked cotton balls on the outside of one of the bags and on top of the ice cube in the bag. Place the second oil-soaked cotton ball on the third plate.

Place one of the clean cotton balls on the outside of the second bag and on top of the ice cube in the bag. Place the second clean cotton ball alongside the oil-soaked cotton ball on the third plate.

Make sure the two cotton balls placed on the ice cubes stay on top of the ice cubes during the experiment. They must remain on the ice cubes for twenty minutes.

73

If they slide off the ice cubes, immediately place them back on top of the ice cubes.

After twenty minutes, feel the clean cotton ball on the third plate. Next feel the clean cotton ball on top of the ice cube. Compare their temperatures.

Next, feel the oil-soaked cotton ball on the third plate and then feel the oil-soaked cotton ball on top of the ice cube. Compare their temperatures.

Observations

Do both clean cotton balls (not soaked in oil) feel about the same temperature? Do both oil-soaked cotton balls feel about the same temperature or does the one that was on the ice cube for twenty minutes feel colder? Does the oil-soaked cotton ball on an ice cube feel colder than the clean cotton ball on an ice cube?

Discussion

Oil spills in the ocean can be harmful to birds and mammals that live or feed in the ocean. These animals can become sick and may even die if they ingest some of the oil floating on the surface. Also, birds can be harmed if their feathers become coated with oil. Mammals too can be harmed if their fur becomes soaked with oil.

There are many small, fluffy feathers, called down feathers, on the underside of a bird's body. These fluffy feathers trap air next to the bird's body, which helps keep the bird warm and also helps the bird float on water.

When a bird becomes coated with oil from an oil spill, oil soaks into the small, fluffy feathers of the bird. These oil-soaked feathers stick together and stick to the body of the bird. When this happens, air that insulates the bird is no longer trapped next to the bird's body, and the bird can freeze to death if the temperature is cold.

When the fur of ocean mammals, such as otters, becomes coated with oil, air that insulates the animal from the cold is no longer trapped next to the animal's

skin. This could cause ocean mammals to freeze to death if the temperature is cold.

Cotton balls are used in this experiment to simulate the small fluffy feathers of birds and the fur of ocean mammals. Cotton balls consist of loosely packed cotton fibers. The loosely packed fibers allow a great deal of air to be trapped in the cotton balls.

You should observe that the two clean cotton balls feel about the same temperature even though one was on an ice cube for twenty minutes. However, you should observe that the oil-soaked cotton ball on the ice cube feels colder than the oil-soaked cotton ball kept on the third plate.

It is difficult for the ice cube to remove heat from the clean cotton ball. That is why the clean cotton ball on the ice cube does not become cold. The clean cotton ball is a poor conductor of heat. A poor conductor of heat is called an insulator.

The air that is trapped inside the clean cotton ball is what makes the clean cotton ball an insulator. Air is a poor conductor of heat. Heat moves slowly through air. This is why it is difficult for the ice cube to remove heat from the clean cotton ball.

The oil-soaked cotton ball on the ice cube becomes cold because the ice cube removes heat from the oil-soaked cotton ball. The oil-soaked cotton ball is a good conductor of heat because oil is a good conductor of heat. When oil was added to the cotton ball, the oil moved into the spaces between the cotton fibers and pushed out the trapped air that was a poor conductor of heat.

Other Things to Try

A bird actually coats its feathers with small amounts of natural oils from special glands on their bodies. These protective oils keep a bird's feathers waterproof. This helps keep the bird afloat on water. If these protective oils are removed from a bird's feathers, the feathers become soaked with water. This could result in the bird losing the insulating layer of air trapped next to its body. Since water is a good conductor of heat, the bird could freeze to death if its fluffy feathers become soaked with water and the temperature is cold.

To show that water is a good conductor of heat, repeat this experiment with a cotton ball soaked with water instead of oil. You should find that a water-soaked cotton ball becomes cold when it is placed on an ice cube.

V. Population and Conservation

It has been estimated that by the year 2000 there will be six billion people alive on the earth. This number is ten times greater than the population of 350 years ago. In other words, for every one person alive in 1650, there are now ten people. All these extra people make great demands on the world's resources.

Populations in developing countries like India, Kenya, and Bangladesh directly depend on renewable resources such as trees, water, and soil. Their increasing populations may use up these environmental resources faster than they can be replenished. Forests are cut for firewood or farming. Loss of ground cover and protective trees causes soil erosion and makes it even more difficult to grow food. Water may be taken from underground aquifers or storage areas faster than it can be replenished.

People in developed or richer countries have a much higher standard of living and use up many more of the world's resources. So as we increase the standard of living in poorer countries, it must be done in ways that do not pollute and destroy our natural resources. We must also change habits in developed countries.

The development of technology can magnify a person's effect on their environment. For example, people in richer countries may produce more pollution because they drive cars rather than ride bicycles. However, technology also gives us a chance to learn, to understand, and to develop new ways to help people and our environment. For example, new technology might lead to developments of solar energy and electric cars that are less polluting.

The following experimental activities will help you learn more about the increasing numbers of people on earth, the effect of overpopulation with limited resources, and ways to conserve our natural resources.

Experiment #14

Can You Model the Population Growth of the World?

Materials

A yardstick   Pennies (117 needed)

Procedure

Lay the yardstick on the floor. The yardstick will represent our scale of time. Each inch will represent 100 years of time.

The beginning of the yardstick will be A.D. 1, the ten-inch mark will be A.D. 1000, sixteen and one-half inches will be 1650, seventeen and one-half inches will be 1750, eighteen and one-half inches will be 1850, nineteen and one-half will be 1950, and twenty inches will represent the year 2000.

Pennies will represent the earth's human population. Each penny will represent one hundred million people. Ten pennies is equivalent to one billion people.

About 2000 years ago in the year A.D. 1, the earth's population is estimated to have been about 200 million. Put two pennies at the beginning of the ruler to represent this population. By the year 1000, the population had increased to about 300 million, so lay three pennies one beside the other on the floor at the ten-inch mark. Don't stack the pennies on top of each other but lay them flat on the floor.

In 1650 the population was about 600 million, so lay six pennies beside one another at the sixteen and one-half mark on the ruler. For populations of 700 million (1750), 1,200 million (1850), and 2,600 million (1950), lay out 7 pennies, 12 pennies, and 28 pennies at the seventeen and one-half, eighteen and one-half, and nineteen and one-half marks, respectively. Finally, it has been estimated that by the year 2000 there will be 6,100 million or 6.1 billion people alive on the earth. To represent this amount lay 61 pennies just to the right of the twenty-inch mark on the ruler.

Observations

Look at your model of the earth's population. What is happening to the population as time passes? Can you estimate the size of our current population? What do you think the population of the earth will be by the year 2050?

Do the changes in population (number of pennies) look like stair steps with equal increases in population for the same time period? Or are the jumps in population getting larger as time passes?

Discussion

From your model, you can tell that the current population is close to six billion people. This population is distributed unevenly among all the countries of the world. For example, the population of the United States in 1990 was about 250 million or one-quarter of a billion people. China's population in 1990 was more than one billion, and India's population was about 800 million. However, Canada, which has more land than either China or India, only had a population of 26 million in 1990. The United Nations has estimated that the population in 2050 will be at least ten billion (100 hundred million) people. This estimate assumes that the earth's population will begin to grow more slowly than in recent years.

Your model shows that the population is increasing. However, it is not increasing like a straight line or a

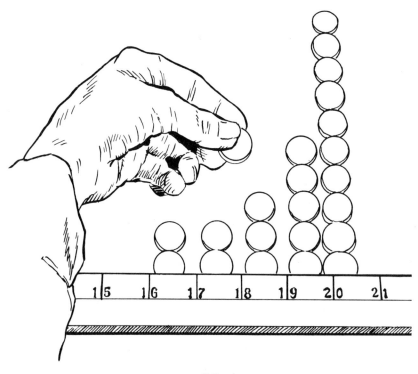

series of stair steps because the amount of increase is becoming greater each year. This type of growth is called exponential growth.

The earth's population is undergoing exponential growth. For example, it took the whole history of humans on earth to reach a population of one billion people around 1830. The population increased to two billion by 1930, just 100 years later. In thirty more years (by 1960), the population increased to three billion. In 1975 the population was four billion. And by 1986, only eleven years later, the population increased to five billion. It took less and less time to add each additional billion to the earth's population. This is an example of exponential growth because the population is increasing faster and faster as time passes.

Population increases for the simple reason that each year more people are being born than are dying. The death rate has decreased because of improved health and control of disease that used to kill many children before they grew to be adults. People are living longer than they did in past history.

The solution to this stress on our biosphere (living things and their environment) must involve people in both poor developing countries and rich developed countries. One part of the solution is for people in developing countries to have fewer numbers of children. Everyone does not need to have the same number of children, but the average needs to be reduced. The second part of the solution is for richer countries to assist the people in poorer countries to increase the quality of their lives. As the quality of life or standard of living increases in a country, the birthrate tends to fall. For example, in 1790 the birthrate in the United States was about eight but now is less than two children per women.

Other Things to Try

Try setting up another model to show the increase in the earth's population for more recent years. You will need a yardstick or ruler and 255 pennies for this model. Use the five-inch mark to represent the year 1950, the six-inch mark to represent 1960, the seven-inch mark to represent the year 1970, the eight-inch mark for 1980, the nine-inch mark for 1990, and the ten-inch mark for the year 2000. Again you will let each penny represent 100 million people.

Use the following population data to construct your model. The population was 26 hundred million in 1950, 30 hundred million in 1960, 37 hundred million in 1970, 48 hundred million in 1980, and 53 hundred million 1990 and should be about 61 hundred million by the year 2000. Use this model to estimate the current population and the population fifty years from now.

Write down some of your ideas on how to provide good quality lives for the people of the world while still maintaining and protecting the earth's environment upon which we all depend.

Experiment #15

How Does Population Change the Food Supply?

Materials

Yeast

Water

Tape

Measuring cups

Two tall, clear glasses

Sugar

A plate

Felt-tip pen

Measuring spoons

Procedure

Place a piece of tape on each glass. Label one glass "less yeast" and the other glass "more yeast." Add one-half cup of water to each glass.

Add one-quarter teaspoon of yeast to the glass labeled "less yeast" and stir with a spoon to mix. Add one teaspoon of yeast to the glass labeled "more yeast" and stir with a spoon to mix.

Add one teaspoon of sugar to each glass and stir the contents of each glass with a spoon to dissolve the sugar in each glass. This may take thirty seconds of stirring.

Place the two glasses on a plate. Place the plate and glasses in a warm spot. A closed window that gets plenty of sunlight is a good place.

Observe the glasses after thirty minutes by tilting

both glasses slightly. Look at that side of the glass that is facing up. You should easily see the gas bubbles rising to the surface. It may help if you observe the tilted glasses with a strong light source, like sunlight, in front of you.

Also observe the amount of foam above the surface of the liquid in each glass. If the foam rises too high and starts to spill out the top of either glass, you can stir the foam back into the liquid with a spoon.

Repeat your observations every hour. Again, look at the foam and look for bubbles rising to the surface in each glass. You will want to continue to observe the glasses each hour until gas bubbles stop forming in one of the glasses. This may take from four to six hours.

Observations

Which glass contains more foam after thirty minutes? When you tilt both glasses, are more bubbles rising to the surface in the glass labeled "less yeast" or in the glass labeled "more yeast?"

After one hour, which glass contains more foam? In which glass are more gas bubbles rising to the surface? After several hours, does the number of gas bubbles rising to the surface decrease in the glass labeled "more yeast?" How long does it take for gas bubbles to stop forming in each glass?

Discussion

In this experiment, you are using yeast to learn how

population can affect the supply of food. Yeast is a simple living system containing one cell. Sugar is a food for yeast. Yeast obtains energy from sugar to live and grow. When yeast obtains energy from sugar, it breaks down the sugar into carbon dioxide gas and ethyl alcohol. The gas bubbles you see rising to the surface in both glasses are the carbon dioxide gas.

Both glasses in this experiment contain the same amount of sugar. The glass labeled "more yeast" contains four times more yeast than the glass labeled "less yeast." The yeast population in the glass labeled "more

yeast" is four times the yeast population in the glass labeled "less yeast."

Four times more yeast are feeding on the sugar in the glass labeled "more yeast" as are feeding on the same amount of sugar in the glass labeled "less yeast." As a result, the sugar in the glass labeled "more yeast" should be consumed faster than the sugar in the glass labeled "less yeast." You can tell in which glass the sugar is being consumed faster by looking at the amount of gas bubbles rising to the surface in each glass.

Eventually, you should see no more gas bubbles forming in the glass labeled "more yeast." This tells you that all the sugar has been consumed in this glass. The yeast have eaten all their available food. The time it takes for the yeast in this glass to completely consume all the sugar in the glass depends on the temperature of the experiment. It may take between four to six hours.

When gas bubbles stop forming in the glass labeled "more yeast," you should notice gas bubbles continue to form in the glass labeled "less yeast." Gas bubbles continue to form in this glass because there is still sugar for the yeast in this glass to feed on.

Although both populations of yeast had the same amount of food at the start of the experiment, the larger yeast population consumed its food supply faster because more yeast were feeding on it. The smaller yeast population consumed its food supply slower because fewer yeast were feeding on it. As a result, the smaller yeast population survived longer.

The food supply and population of a particular species of plant or animal are usually balanced. Food supply is a major force that limits the population of species. Changes in the food supply can cause the population of a species to change. An increase in the food supply may support a larger population, while a decrease in the food supply may cause a decrease in the population.

Human population is also limited by the amount of food available. Until the 1800s, the population of the world increased only slightly over thousands of years. Limited food supplies and lack of health care were causes of slow growth in human population.

In the 1800s and early 1900s, advanced farming techniques were developed and food production increased. More food became available for more people, and the population started to increase quickly. Improved health care has also contributed to population growth.

Other Things to Try

When gas bubbles stop forming in the glass labeled "more yeast," continue to observe the formation of gas bubbles in the glass labeled "less yeast." How much longer do gas bubbles continue to form in this glass?

Experiment #16

How Can People Help Conserve Energy Resources?

Materials

Household bills for electricity or natural gas

Procedure

You will need the permission and help of an adult in your household to carry out this activity. You will compare energy costs before and after conserving energy.

Try to think of ways that you and the other people that live in your household can conserve or use less energy. You could turn out lights when you leave a room. You could turn the thermostat to a lower temperature setting in winter to use less energy for heating. You could turn up the thermostat to a higher temperature setting in summer to use less energy for cooling.

Your household heating may come from electricity, natural gas, heating oil, propane, coal, wood, or kerosene. If you have electricity or natural gas for heating, you may get monthly bills that include this expense. For the other types of heating, you may have to compare the amount of fuel used for a longer period of time, such as the winter of one year to the next.

Try these ways or others you can think of to save

energy. The methods you use will be different at different times of the year. Compare the monthly bills before and after you try to conserve energy.

Observations

How many kilowatt hours of electricity were used in your household before you tried conserving electricity? How many kilowatt hours of electricity were used in your household after you began trying to conserve electricity?

If you have natural gas where you live, how many cubic feet of natural gas were used in your household before you began conserving energy? How many cubic

feet of natural gas were used in your household after you began trying to conserve electricity?

Discussion

When we study living things, we have to remember to study humans and how we affect the planet. There are many ways we can waste or save the earth's resources. In this experiment, we explore one way we can avoid wasting energy resources. What each person does can make a difference in the future of our earth's environment.

Households in the United States use a great deal of energy in the forms of electricity and sometimes natural gas or other fuel. Energy is used for heating, cooling, refrigeration, lighting, and household appliances. Electrical energy is measured in kilowatt hours. Burning a hundred-watt light bulb for ten hours would require one kilowatt hour of electricity since kilo means one thousand.

One way to supply our future energy needs is to build more electrical generating plants. These plants may use the power of falling water to turn generators. Or they may burn coal or use heat energy from the nuclei of atoms to change water to steam and use the steam to turn generators that produce electricity. Another way to help meet our future energy needs is to reduce the amount of energy we use in our daily lives. Most likely, in the future, we will need to do both these things. However, before we build more plants to produce energy, we should make sure we are not wasting what we have.

The results of each household will be different from each other and change from one month to the next depending on the season of the year. However, you should find that you can lower the amount of energy used in your household. You are saving energy. Saving energy or using our natural resources wisely is sometimes called conservation. Conserving our natural resources means we are concerned about our earth and the future.

Turning off the lights that are not needed can save electricity. It is estimated that one-fifth of household electricity goes for lighting. We may not think of electricity as having an environmental effect, but the energy to produce that electricity must be produced somewhere. If a coal-burning plant is used, then carbon dioxide, a greenhouse gas, and sulfur dioxide, a cause of acid rain, are produced. One light bulb may not seem to make much difference. However, there are about 100 million households in the United States, so our combined effects can be tremendous.

Other Things to Try

The activity of conserving our energy resources is one you can continue for the rest of your life. Compare energy bills for three months prior to trying to conserve energy and for three months after trying to conserve energy.

See if an adult in your household would replace burned out incandescent bulbs with compact fluorescent bulbs. ONLY AN ADULT SHOULD PUT IN OR TAKE OUT LIGHT BULBS. Compact fluorescent light bulbs screw into regular incandescent light sockets. Incandescent bulbs are the type that get quite hot. Compact fluorescent bulbs stay fairly cool and so use less than a fourth of the energy required for incandescent bulbs. Fluorescent bulbs cost more to buy, but they last ten times as long and pay for themselves in electricity savings.

Many utility companies have information brochures on saving energy and some even examine homes for ways to save electricity. Maybe your household can get additional information on ways to save energy. Some possible ways for you and an adult to save energy and money in your household include insulating around the edges of windows and doors, turning down water heater temperature, turning off heat and air conditioning in rooms not being used, planting trees to shade homes in summer, drying clothes in the sun, making sure heating air filters are clean, making sure heaters are adjusted to maximum efficiency, and dressing warmer in winter so rooms do not need to be kept as warm.

Complete List of Materials Used in These Experiments

A
aluminum foil
ant
apples

B
bags, zipper-
close plastic
baking soda
board, small
wooden
bowl, large

C
closet, dark
cooking oil
cotton balls
cup, measuring
cup, styrofoam

F
fertilizer

G
glasses, tall clear
grass, growing

H
household
electricity
bills
hydrogen
peroxide

I
ice cubes

J
jars, large clear
glass
jars, small glass

K
knife

L
land with living
things
land with rocks
or logs
leaf, dead, dried-
out
leaves, fresh
green

M
marker
match
match box

P
paper
paper towel
pen, felt-tip
pencil
pennies
plates

potato

R
ryegrass seed

S
sand, white
scissors
shovel, small
spinach leaves
spoon, long-
handled
metal
spoon,
measuring
sugar

T
Tabasco sauce
tape
trowel

V
vegetable peeler
vinegar

W
water

Y
yard stick
yeast

Index